GRAPHIC WORKS
OF THE
AMERICAN
THIRTIES

GRAPHIC WORKS OF THE AMERICAN THIRTIES

A BOOK OF 100 PRINTS

A DA CAPO PAPERBACK

ISBN: 0-306-80078-0

First Paperback Edition 1977

This DaCapo Press paperback edition of *Graphic Works of the American Thirties*
is an unabridged republication of *America Today: A Book of 100 Prints* published
in New York in 1936 by the American Artists' Congress.

Published by Da Capo Press, Inc.
A Subsidiary of Plenum Publishing Corporation
227 West 17th Street
New York, New York 10011

INTRODUCTION

THE ORIGIN OF THESE PRINTS

In bringing together the prints reproduced in this volume the American Artists' Congress has made an important contribution to the new movement now manifest in the graphic arts in this country.

The one hundred prints here reproduced were selected from hundreds submitted by artists in all parts of the United States in response to the announcement by the Congress of a nation-wide exhibition of duplicate exhibits to be held simultaneously in thirty American cities during the month of December, 1936. The jury was composed of the following artists: Arnold Blanch, Stuart Davis, Ernest Fiene, Hugo Gellert, William Gropper, Wanda Gág, Yasuo Kuniyoshi, Margaret Lowengrund, Louis Lozowick, George Picken, Harry Sternberg, Lynd Ward, Max Weber. Each juror was asked to include one of his own works in the exhibition. The method of selection was an innovation in jury procedure. It was the most democratic available. Each juror made an individual selection of one hundred prints, and then their written lists were tallied for the hundred prints receiving the highest number of votes.

The exhibition, as a whole, may be characterized as "socially-conscious". It reflects a deep-going change that has been taking place among artists for the last few years— a change that has taken many of them not only to their studio window to look outside, but right through the door and into the street, into the mills, farms, mines and factories. More and more artists are finding the world outside their studios increasingly interesting and exciting, and filling their pictures with their reactions to humanity about them, rather than with apples or flowers. Even in the case of artists who have been working in abstract design, it is interesting to note their concern with social issues and subjects, at least as a source of inspiration, as indicated by their titles.

This revolutionary change occuring among artists has a complement in the changing attitude of a growing public toward the print. Many are learning to appreciate the fine possibilities inherent in this medium for humor, tragedy, satire, and full-bodied depiction of life. They no longer regard the print only as wall decoration, but as a form of contemporary expression, whether it be hung on the wall or studied in portfolio. And as more people embrace this new attitude and interest, more artists under-

5

stand the importance of making their work accessible to this larger public. They realize that it is as wrong to destroy a fine plate or block after pulling a small number of proofs, when thousands of people would like to own such prints, as it is to create an artificial scarcity of food by destroying pigs and wheat while hundreds of thousands go hungry.

In arranging for the simultaneous showing of these thirty duplicate exhibitions, the American Artists' Congress is attempting to help the artist reach a public comparable in size to that of the book and motion picture, and to bring the artist and public closer together by making the print relevant to the life of the people, and financially accessible to the person of small means. It is trying to bring about that healthy interaction between artist and public which alone can develop a great popular movement in American art, and re-establish the high traditions of such masters of the print as Dürer, Callot, Rembrandt, Goya, Hogarth, and Daumier.

ALEX R. STAVENITZ.

THESE PRINTS AND THE PUBLIC

The American Artists' Congress, in this, its first, national exhibition of contemporary American prints, presents an issue of far reaching importance to the American public.

Shall the American artist manage the production, distribution and education in the field in which he is a specialist, or shall he continue to be the pawn of various lay agencies which have neglected or used him in the past for reasons dictated sometimes by idealism, sometimes by whim, sometimes by profit, or social prestige?

The artist needs autonomy. He can assert autonomy, as he has in this exhibit, but he cannot make such an assertion effective without public support.

In 1910 the Chicago Society of Etchers inaugurated autonomous action by artists in this country by staging its own exhibitions and publishing its own books and print editions. Similar efforts were undertaken by the Brooklyn Society of Etchers, the California Society of Printmakers and other organizations. The American Designers Gallery and the American Union of Decorative Artists and Craftsmen made brave attempts at such management in 1928.

The American Artists' Congress and its varied program is the result of cumulative pressure toward constructive action to satisfy a deep-lying cultural need, accelerated by the depression. Direct contact between the layman who uses or might use

6

works of art and the individual artist who produces them, together with the recognition of the artist's authority to choose and manage his own exhibits, is a healthy and fruitful condition. The present divorce of user and producer, encouraged and fostered by middlemen, for whom there is a specious respect, is an unhealthy and constricting condition.

By direct contact with his audience the artist avoids the censorships proceeding from both the profit motive and lay officialdom. He also gains the inspiration which arises from a sense of usefulness, which is inherent in that contact. Responsibility for the support or neglect of his work is placed squarely where it belongs—on the community. No honest mind of maturity and strength needs more nourishing, beyond the physical, than the challenge of this condition. The Government Arts Projects, in addition to the necessary physical support, provide such direct contact and elimination of middlemen (except where they have drawn in lay art officials as regional directors). This characteristic distinguishes the Government program as one of the most significant steps in building a national culture ever undertaken by the American people. The artist, for the first time in our history, has his chance to produce with the sure knowledge that his work will be used by the society in which he lives.

The advantages to the general public of this direct contact are no less important. Art is taken out of the studio, the gallery and the art museum and put to work in the homes and public buildings of everyday. The artist ceases to be an ornament of the pink-tea, a playboy companion of the dilettante patron, a remote hero with a famous name. He becomes, instead, a workman among workers. He paints murals on a scaffold of planks and ladders. He prints his etchings, lithographs or woodblocks with hands which know ink and the rollers and wheels of his press. He works. He produces. He lives.

RALPH M. PEARSON.

THE WOODCUT

The oldest example of this, the earliest form of engraving—which has been used by the Chinese for over a thousand years—is from the middle of the ninth century, A.D. But the woodcut as we know it, first appeared in the middle of the fifteenth century. It very quickly became more popular than any pictorial medium then in use, among the common people. Which is a marked contrast to the present day limited and signed proofs for the dealer, collector and speculator in fine prints.

The list of artists who have made woodcuts, from Dürer to our own day, is a very long one. A preoccupation in the eighteenth century with the engraved metal plate was followed by a revival in the following century and a subsequent decadence into magazine illustration. With the invention of photography and photo-engraving for reproduction on a mass scale, the woodcut almost ceased to exist. During this low ebb, small groups of artists on the continent and in America kept the craft alive until at the turn of the present century, a new interest burst forth. Today, a great tradition in the art of the woodcut is being established.

Technically, the woodcut requires not only a knowledge of drawing but skill in a distinct kind of craftsmanship. Much more than "hacking" at the wood is necessary. Clarity in design and expression in both line and area are most important. The wood-*cut* is done on soft wood, the long-grain plank of apple, pear, beech, cherry—and also linoleum. All woods used are type-high, planed flat and sandpapered very smooth. The design is either drawn directly or traced upon the block, and the method, roughly, is to cut away all white or light areas, leaving the black lines and areas raised, so that, when inked, they will print on paper under pressure. A knife or carver is used for incising the line and chisels or similar tools are used to clean out superfluous wood.

In wood *engraving* a hard, closely-grained wood—such as box or maple—is used. The block is cut across the grain of the tree, and an entirely different set of tools must be employed—burins or gravers and tint tools of different sizes and shapes whose capacities for varying degrees of fine lines and large spaces allow more profuse tonal and color variations than is possible in the woodcut.

Printing, as in all the graphic arts, requires a great deal of skill. Perhaps the best method is with the Washington-Franklin proofing press, or the flat-bed press. But good proofs have been made with the burnisher, the back of a spoon, a Japanese baren, a roller, the old-fashioned letter press—and even the foot.

H. GLINTENKAMP.

ETCHING

Etching is printing from an acid-incised, inked plate. It was first done early in 1500; Daniel Hopfer is generally considered to have been the first known etcher. Albrecht Dürer, who produced etchings only a few years later, was the first important artist to use this medium. The first plates were of iron; red-lead was used for stopping out: the prints were pulled in wooden presses. These great technical handicaps were magnificently overcome. Modern etchers command not only superior metals, standardized acids and grounds, but also, in the steel-plating process, the means of overcoming the wearing-away of the metal itself.

The mediums of art have certain innate qualities. No one would think of doing small easel paintings in fresco, just as no sensitive artist would think of doing a water color on an etching plate (miscalled colored etchings). And basically, because it is a reproductive medium, etching is meant for wide distribution.

The incisiveness of the bitten line demands that something be said with that line. The greatest masters of black and white have used the medium naturally and normally, line and tone telling the artist's reaction to his time. The prints were widely distributed and sold cheaply. For the most part the plates were used until they began to wear down.

Rembrandt's sympathetic renderings of the Jew, Goya's moving depictions of the horrors of war, Forain's sympathetic pictures of the people and his caustic criticism of the courts, Hogarth's biting comment on the morals of his time, and a host of others are examples of great artists utilizing the normal function of this medium.

Lately the print has been perverted into a false, unhealthy, unnatural preciocity. What is said—with tools an artist devotes a lifetime to master—has become unimportant. The plate itself is deliberately destroyed, sometimes only after ten proofs have been pulled, in order that rarity may be the chief selling point. Prints become a display of technical acrobatics, as meaningless and functionless as a tightrope walker juggling twelve balls at once. And people are cunningly mislead into paying two or three hundred dollars for such a print, while a good Daumier or Goya can be gotten for twenty dollars.

Society has forced the artist into playing this game, into trying to catch with special tricks, special techniques and especially limited editions, the eye of the few who can pay. Such perversions have resulted in the spiritual death of many artists and almost in the death of graphic art.

Fortunately, some artists have been forced, by the none too gentle jolts of the times, to open their eyes. They have awakened to the realization that they have lost touch with actual life. As a result, prints are now being produced that portray the vital aspects of contemporary life. Editions are now unlimited. Prices are now low—not low enough yet—but even so more available to the huge new audience.

The hundred prints in this book move in this direction. They represent the beginning of a renaissance of graphic art.

HARRY STERNBERG.

9

LITHOGRAPHY

Lithography is the youngest of the graphic arts. It was invented about a century ago by Aloys Senefelder (1771-1834).

Reduced to simplest terms, the lithographic process consists of the following steps: (a) drawing with grease-containing pencil, crayon or ink on a flat surface of limestone; (b) chemical treatment of the stone (weak solution of nitric acid) so that the parts covered by the drawing are made receptive to ink and impervious to water, while, contrariwise, parts unoccupied by any drawing become receptive to water but impervious to ink; (c) feeding to the stone the ink, which is absorbed and repelled in the manner indicated; (d) putting the stone in a press and transferring the drawing to paper.

From the standpoint of technical procedure, lithography is the most flexible graphic art. Its great virtue is the range of tone which it makes accessible to the artist —from the softest, most delicate grays to the deepest, richest blacks, which are given a specific, textural quality by the surface of the stone. The finest line of etching, the grain of aquatint, the bold strokes of woodcut, the transparency of wash—all are attainable by the practised lithographer. A slight hint of the limitless possibilities for experiment in this medium is afforded by a careful examination of the mutually differing lithographs by Biddle, Kent, Kuniyoshi, Gropper, Gag, Dehn, Fiene, Davis and others.

A knowledge of the medium, and a mastery of technique, when combined with a gift for formal organization, will distinguish the work of talent from the work of mediocrity. But nothing could be more sterile than exclusive preoccupation with technical experimentation, and nothing more foreign to the best traditions of the graphic arts. During the Reformation, the French Revolution, the American Civil War, the Russian Revolution, the graphic artist played a tremendous role—with no detriment to his art. Certainly Dürer's wood and metal engravings, or Daumier's lithographs and woodcuts, are no less valuable plastically because they were used in the service of an idea.

This is especially important to remember now, when progress and reaction are contending throughout the world. The integrity of the artist and the very fate of art are threatened today. If, by a formally significant creative interpretation, the artist fastens the attention of his contemporaries upon a living issue, he continues in the present the work of the great graphic artists of the past.

LOUIS LOZOWICK.

10

A CHECK-LIST OF THE ARTISTS

Plate 1
SPRING TWILIGHT by J. J. Lankes. *Woodcut, 9⅛ x 8.*

Plate 2
CORN FIELD by Doris Lee. *Lithograph, 6⅞ x 9¾.*

Plate 3
PROVINCETOWN by Louis G. Ferstadt. *Lithograph, 8⅞ x 12, edition of 50.*

Plate 4
BACKYARD ROMANCE by George Jo Mess. *Aquatint, 7⅞ x 6⅞, edition of 50.*

Plate 5
LANDSFORD, PA. by Riva Helfond. *Lithograph, 10 x 13¾, edition of 35.*

Plate 6
THE HAY MEADOW by Fiske Boyd. *Woodcut, 8 x 11⅝, edition of 100.*

Plate 7
A. T. and T. by Karl Metzler. *Lithograph, 9⅜ x 14, edition of 40.*

Plate 8
GLOUCESTER DOCKS by John Lonergan. *Lithograph, 9¾ x 12, edition of 40.*

Plate 9
SUNDAY ON THE WATERFRONT by Charles Surendorf. *Linoleum block, 8 x 10.*

Plate 10
UNDERPASS by Coreen Mary Spellman. *Mezzotint, 4¾ x 7⅛, edition unlimited.*

Plate 11
POWERHOUSE by Salvatore Pinto. *Wood engraving, 8 7/16 x 7 11/16, edition of 50.*

Plate 12
ROCK ISLAND YARDS by Bob White. *Etching, 7 x 9, edition unlimited.*

Plate 13
EAST RIVER LANDSCAPE by George Picken. *Lithograph, 8½ x 12⅞, edition of 35.*

Plate 14
TUG BOATS by I. J. Sanger. *Wood engraving, 6⅞ x 4⅞, edition of 50.*

Plate 15
MANHATTAN BACKYARDS by H. Glintenkamp. *Wood engraving, 7⅛ x 5⅛, edition of 50.*

Plate 16
BRACING SUBWAY EXCAVATION by Abbo Ostrowsky. *Etching, 13⅝ x 10¾.*

Plate 17
VENUS OF 23RD STREET by Joseph Solman. *Linoleum cut, 9⅞ x 4¾, edition unlimited.*

Plate 18
FACTORY DISTRICT by Will Barnet. *Lithograph, 8⅞ x 10⅞.*

Plate 19
PROGRESS by Wanda Gág. *Lithograph, 8⅛ x 11⅞, edition unlimited.*

Plate 20
MOONLIT INTERIOR by Hobson Pittman. *Woodcut, 9⅞ x 7⅞, edition of 60.*

Plate 21
TRAFFIC CONTROL by Benton Spruance. *Lithograph, 8¾ x 14⅜, edition of 35.*

Plate 22
AMERICA AND ITS PEOPLE by Ralph M. Rosenborg. *Linoleum cut, 9 x 12, edition of 50.*

Plate 23
ADOBE BRICK MAKER by Kenneth M. Adams. *Lithograph, 9¼ x 9⅞, edition of 50.*

Plate 24
PEASANT WOMAN by Victor De Wilde. *Etching, 11⅝ x 7⅞.*

Plate 25
NORTH CAROLINA MOUNTAIN WOMAN by Barbara Latham. *Wood engraving, 8 x 10, edition of 35.*

Plate 26
THE HARVEST — SOUTH CAROLINA by Charles Pollack. *Lithograph, 9⅞ x 14, edition of 35.*

Plate 27
CITY MARKET — CHARLESTOWN by Andrée Ruellan. *Lithograph, 8⅞ x 12⅞, edition of 40.*

Plate 28
YOUNG GIRL WITH BOY by Ione Robinson. *Lithograph, 14 x 10.*

Plate 29
MOTHER by Robert V. Neuman. *Linoleum cut, 11⅛ x 8⅜.*

Plate 30
PENSIONED by Max Weber, *Woodcut, 4¼ x 1⅞.*

Plate 31
THE SHREW by Lucile Blanch. *Lithograph, 9½ x 13½, edition of 50.*

Plate 32
LA TOILETTE by Doris Spiegal. *Copper engraving, 3½ x 4⅜, edition of 100.*

Plate 33
STORY OF THE FLOOD by Larry C. Rodda. *Lithograph, 9⅞ x 13⅞, edition of 30.*

Plate 34
DERELICTS by Mabel Dwight. *Lithograph, 9¾ x 13⅜.*

Plate 35
STEVEDORES by Beatrice Cuming. *Etching, 8⅞ x 11, edition unlimited.*

Plate 36
THE STOKERS by Irwin D. Hoffman. *Etching, 8 x 10¹³⁄₁₆, edition of 100.*

Plate 37
PORTRAIT OF A MINER by Philip Evergood. *Etching on steel, 7⅜ x 6⅜, edition of 30.*

Plate 38
WATERFRONT by Saul. *Etching, 4 x 5⅞, edition of 50.*

Plate 39
BAR ROOM by Bennet Buck. *Drypoint, 6⁷⁄₁₆ x 7⅛, edition unlimited.*

Plate 40
SHORE LEAVE by Paul Cadmus. *Etching, 10⅜ x 11½, edition of 50.*

Plate 41
CARNIVAL by Don Glasell. *Etching, 7⁵⁄₁₆ x 9⁵⁄₁₆, edition of 30.*

Plate 42
SIDE SHOW—CONEY ISLAND by M. Lois Murphy. *Wood engraving, 9 x 7, edition of 60.*

Plate 43
CIRCUS by Anne Steele Marsh, *Wood engraving, 8 x 10.*

Plate 44
SHOOTING GALLERY by Angelo Pinto. *Wood engraving, 6¾ x 8½, edition of 50.*

Plate 45
FROM THE BOARDWALK by Yasuo Kuniyoshi. *Lithograph, 13¾ x 9⅛, edition of 45.*

Plate 46
LIGHTS by Fritz Eichenberg. *Wood engraving, 6¼ x 4¹³⁄₁₆.*

Plate 47
DANCERS RESTING by Raphael Soyer. *Lithograph, 10¾ x 8¾, edition unlimited.*

Plate 48
THE LINDY HOP by Miguel Covarrubias. *Lithograph, 13 x 9½, edition unlimited.*

Plate 49
SOUTHERN MOUNTAINEER by Howard Cook. *Aquatint, 11⅞ x 9, edition of 35.*

Plate 50
CALLA LILY by Kalman Kubinyi. *Drypoint 9⁹⁄₁₆ x 7½.*

Plate 51
COAL TOWN by Barbara Burrage. *Woodcut, 11½ x 9, edition unlimited.*

Plate 52
SPRING by Victor Candell. *Linoleum cut, 9⅞ x 8⅛, edition of 50.*

Plate 53
COAL GATHERERS by Winifred Milius. *Woodcut, 5 x 3¾₆, edition unlimited.*

Plate 54
THE COAL PICKERS by Harry Gottlieb. *Lithograph, 10 x 13⅞.*

Plate 55
BLACK LEGION WIDOW by Maurice Merlin. *Linoleum block, 8 x 6.*

Plate 56
BEHIND THE BANDWAGON by Honoré Guilbeau. *Etching, 6⅞ x 10, edition of 50.*

Plate 57
AFTER THE HARVEST by Chet La More. *Lithograph, 9¾ x 13⅝, edition of 30.*

Plate 58
HURRICANE by Eugene Morley. *Lithograph, 9½ x 13⅛, edition of 35.*

Plate 59
SAND! by George Biddle. *Lithograph, 9¹³₁₆ x 13⅞, edition of 50.*

Plate 60
DUSTBOWL by Abramovitz. *Wood engraving, 7⅞ x 9¹⁵₁₆.*

Plate 61
DUST by Mervin Jules. *Lithograph, 7¼ x 13⅞, edition of 30.*

Plate 62
THE DROUGHT by Fred Nagler. *Etching, 11⅛ x 10½, edition of 100.*

Plate 63
REFORESTATION by Helen West Heller. *Woodcut, 11⅛ x 9¾.*

Plate 64
THE APPLE MAN by Olle Nordmark. *Wood engraving, 6 x 4¹³₁₆, edition of 35.*

Plate 65
SUN AND DUST by LeRoy Flint. *Aquatint, 6¹³₁₆ x 8¹³₁₆, edition of 50.*

Plate 66
LAND OF PLENTY by Lucienne Bloch. *Woodcut, 10⅝ x 8¾.*

Plate 67
VILLAGE by Harry Hering. *Aquatint, 9 x 10⅝, edition of 35.*

Plate 68
DESERTED FARM by Arnold Blanch. *Lithograph, 9½ x 14¼, edition of 35.*

Plate 69
COAL MINING TOWN by Harry Sternberg. *Lithograph, 9½ x 14.*

Plate 70
BOOTLEG MINING, PENNA. by Elizabeth Olds. *Lithograph, 9⅞ x 13⅞.*

Plate 71
COAL PICKERS by Margaret Lowengrund. *Etching, 9⅞ x 13¹³₁₆.*

Plate 72
RUST COTTON PICKER COMES TO THE SOUTH by Shelby Shackelford. *Linoleum cut, 12¾ x 9¾.*

Plate 73
WORKER RESTING by Edward Landon. *Linoleum cut, 4¼ x 8⅞.*

Plate 74
THREE MEN ON A BENCH by Louis Schanker. *Woodcut, 7 x 12⁷₁₆.*

Plate 75
VETERAN by Irving Marantz. *Woodcut, 10 x 8.*

Plate 76
THE BOOTBLACK'S NIGHTMARE by Alex R. Stavenitz. *Aqua-mezzotint, 11⅝ x 8⁹₁₆, edition unlimited.*

Plate 77
HIGH COST OF LIVING by Anton Refregier. *Lithograph, 7⅝ x 10¼, edition of 50.*

Plate 78
CRIERS IN THE WILDERNESS by Lewis C. Daniel. *Drypoint, 8⅞ x 11¹³₁₆, edition of 50.*

Plate 79
GOSSIP by Hugh C. Miller. *Aquatint, 9⅞ x 11⅞, edition of 30.*

13

Plate 80
DETECTIVES AND GANGSTERS by Russell T. Limbach. *Lithograph, 6¼ x 13¹³⁄₁₆, edition of 40.*

Plate 81
DICTATION by Jack Markow. *Lithograph, 7½ x 9¾.*

Plate 82
PIECES OF SILVER by Hugo Gellert. *Lithograph, 12¾ x 11½, edition of 50.*

Plate 83
BASEBALL TEAM by Aline Fruhauf. *Collotype, 7 x 14, edition of 400.*

Plate 84
RELIGION by Lamar Baker. *Lithograph, 11½ x 8¾.*

Plate 85
MINE SUPERINTENDENT by Ernest Fiene. *Lithograph, 8¹⁄₁₆ x 11⁵⁄₁₆, edition of 100.*

Plate 86
ROADS by Jolan Gross Bettelheim. *Lithograph, 12¾ x 9¹³⁄₁₆, edition of 30.*

Plate 87
INSANE ASYLUM by Bernard Sanders. *Etching, 7¹⁄₁₆ x 4¹³⁄₁₆.*

Plate 88
IT CAN'T HAPPEN HERE by Werner Drewes. *Linoleum cut, 6 x 10³⁄₁₆.*

Plate 89
14TH STREET by José M. Pavon. *Lithograph, 9¾ x 13⅝.*

Plate 90
A MANHATTAN LANDSCAPE WITH FIGURES by Ida Abelman. *Lithograph, 13⅞ x 9⅝, edition of 50.*

Plate 91
AMERICAN SCENF by J. B. Turnbull. *Lithograph, 14 x 10.*

Plate 92
STRIKE by Emory Ladanyi. *Linoleum cut, 10¼ x 6½, edition unlimited.*

Plate 93
DAWN IN THE ASSEMBLY by Don Freeman. *Lithograph, 9⁷⁄₁₆ x 12¾, edition of 33.*

Plate 94
TROUBLE IN FRISCO by Fletcher Martin. *Offset lithography, 11¼ diameter, edition of 150.*

Plate 95
LET 'EM EAT CAKE by Dorothy Rutka. *Aquatint, 7¹³⁄₁₆ x 6¼, edition of 50.*

Plate 96
ROAD WORKERS by William Gropper. *Lithograph, 12½ x 9⅝, edition of 75.*

Plate 97
IN TIMES OF PEACE by Morris Topchevsky. *Aquatint, 8⁷⁄₁₆ x 7⁷⁄₁₆, edition of 40.*

Plate 98
LYNCHING by Louis Lozowick. *Lithograph, 10¼ x 7¼.*

Plate 99
COMPANY TOWN by Lynd Ward. *Wood engraving, 5 x 4½, edition unlimited.*

Plate 100
AND NOW WHERE? by Rockwell Kent. *Lithograph, 13⅛ x 9⅜, edition unlimited.*

14

AMERICA TODAY

1
Spring Twilight
J. J. Lankes

2
Corn Field
Doris Lee

3
Provincetown
Louis G. Ferstadt

4
Backyard Romance
George Jo Mess

5
Landsford, Pa.
Riva Helfond

6
The Hay Meadow
Fiske Boyd

7
A. T. and T.
Karl Metzler

8
Gloucester Docks
John Lonergan

9
Sunday on the Water Front
Charles Surendorf

10
Underpass
Coreen Mary Spellman

O·59

11
Powerhouse
Salvatore Pinto

12
Rock Island Yards
Bob White

13
East River Landscape
George Picken

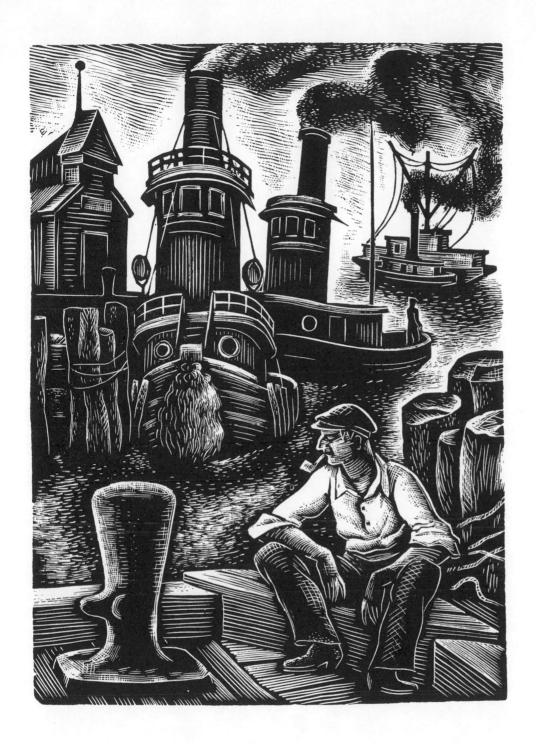

14
Tug Boats
I. J. Sanger

15
Manhattan Backyards
H. Glintenkamp

16
Bracing Subway Excavation
Abbo Ostrowsky

17
Venus of 23rd Street
Joseph Solman

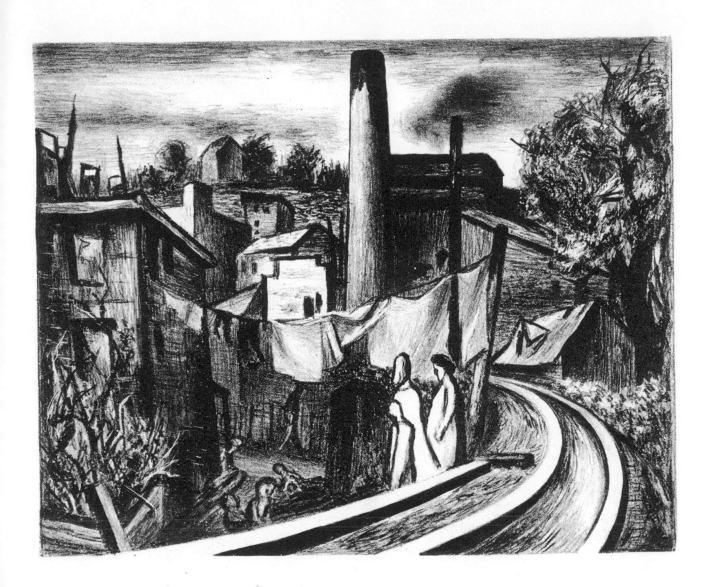

18
Factory District
Will Barnet

19
Progress
Wanda Gág

20
Moonlit Interior
Hobson Pittman

21
Traffic Control
Benton Spruance

22
America and its People
Ralph M. Rosenborg

23
Adobe Brick Maker
Kenneth M. Adams

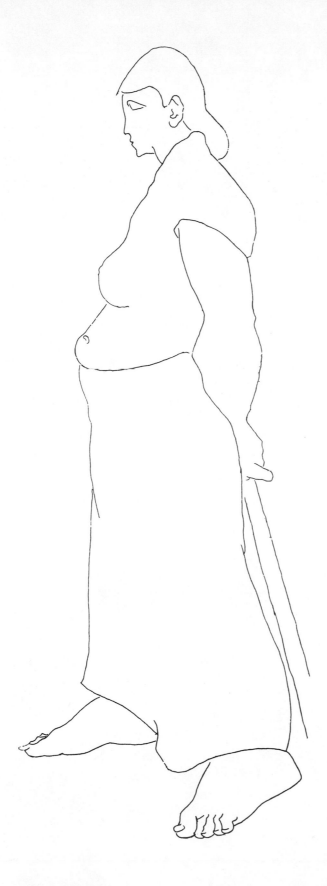

24
Peasant Woman
Victor De Wilde

North Carolina Mountain Woman
Barbara Latham

26
The Harvest—South Carolina
Charles Pollock

27
City Market—Charlestown
Andrée Ruellan

28
Young Girl With Boy
Ione Robinson

29
Mother
Robert V. Neuman

30
Pensioned
Max Weber

31
The Shrew
Lucile Blanch

D. Spiegel

32
La Toilette
Doris Spiegal

Story of the Flood
Larry C. Rodda

54
Derelicts
Mabel Dwight

35
Stevedores
Beatrice Cuming

36
The Stokers
Irwin D. Hoffman

Portrait of a Miner
Philip Evergood

38
Waterfront
Saul

39
Bar Room
Bennet Buck

40
Shore Leave
Paul Cadmus

41
Carnival
Don Glasell

42
Side Show
M. Lois Murphy

43
Circus
Anne Steele Marsh

Shooting Gallery
Angelo Pinto

45
From the Boardwalk
Yasuo Kuniyoshi

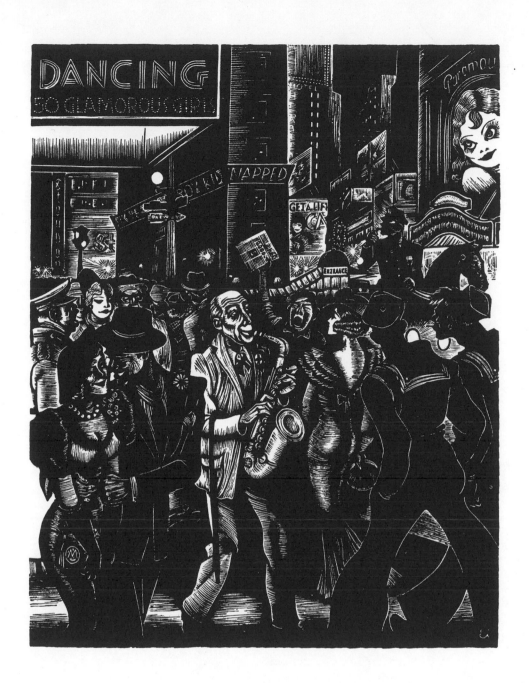

46
Lights
Fritz Eichenberg

47
Dancers Resting
Raphael Soyer

48
The Lindy Hop
Miguel Covarrubias

49
Southern Mountaineer
Howard Cook

50
Calla Lily
Kalman Kubinyi

51
Coal Town
Barbara Burrage

52
Spring
Victor Candell

53
Coal Gatherers
Winifred Milius

54
The Coal Pickers
Harry Gottlieb

55
Black Legion Widow
Maurice Merlin

56
Behind the Band Wagon
Honoré Guilbeau

57
After the Harvest
Chet La More

Hurricane
Eugene Morley

59
Sand!
George Biddle

60
Dustbowl
Abromovitz

61
Dust
Mervin Jules

62
The Drought
Fred Nagler

63
Reforestation
Helen West Heller

64
The Apple Man
Olle Nordmark

65
Sun and Dust
Le Roy Flint

66
Land of Plenty
Lucienne Bloch

67
Village
Harry Hering

68
Deserted Farm
Arnold Blanch

69
Coal Mining Town
Harry Sternberg

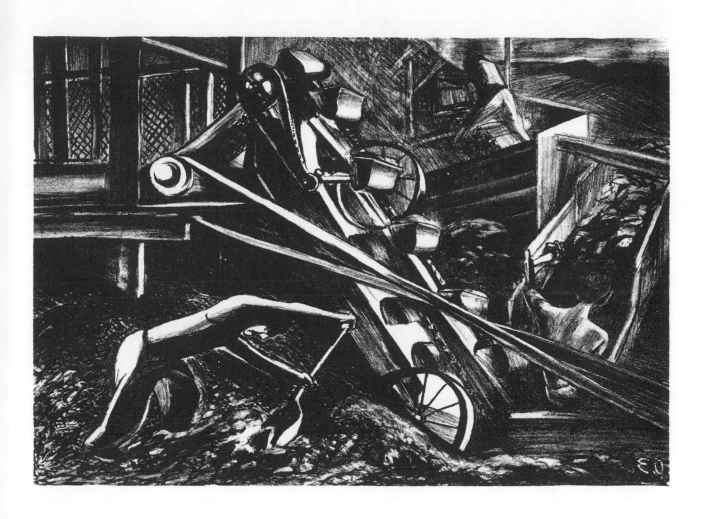

70
"Bootleg" Mining, Penna.
Elizabeth Olds

71
Coal Pickers
Margaret Lowengrund

72
Rust Cotton Picker Comes to the South
Shelby Shackleford

73
Worker Resting
Edward Landon

74
Three Men on Bench
Louis Schanker

75
Veteran
Irving Marantz

76
The Bootblack's Nightmare
Alex R. Stavenitz

77
High Cost of Living
Anton Refregier

78
Criers in the Wilderness
Lewis C. Daniel

79
Gossip
Hugh C. Miller

Detectives and Gangsters
Russell T. Limbach

81
Dictation
Jack Markow

82
Pieces of Silver
Hugo Gellert

83
Baseball Team
Aline Fruhauf

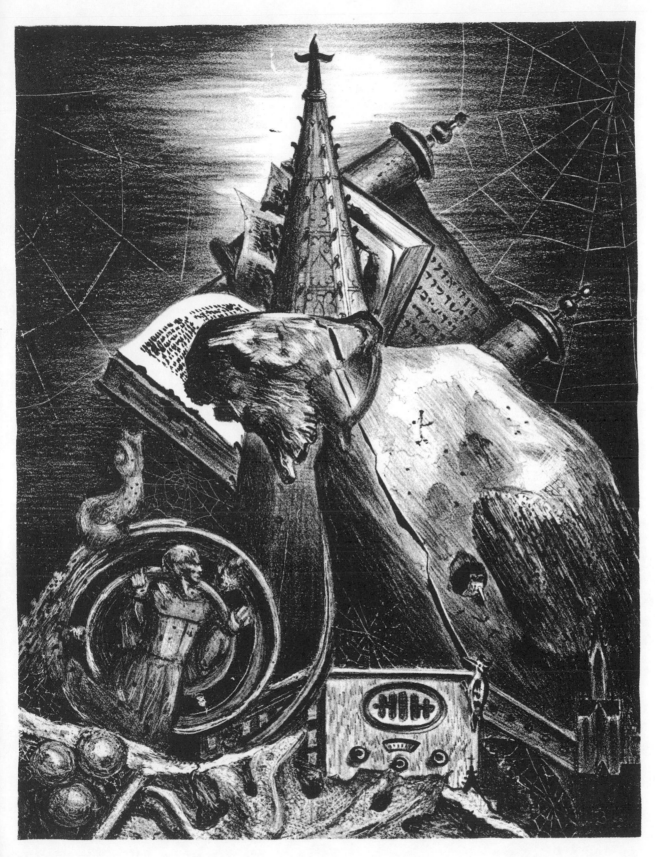

84
Religion
Lamar Baker

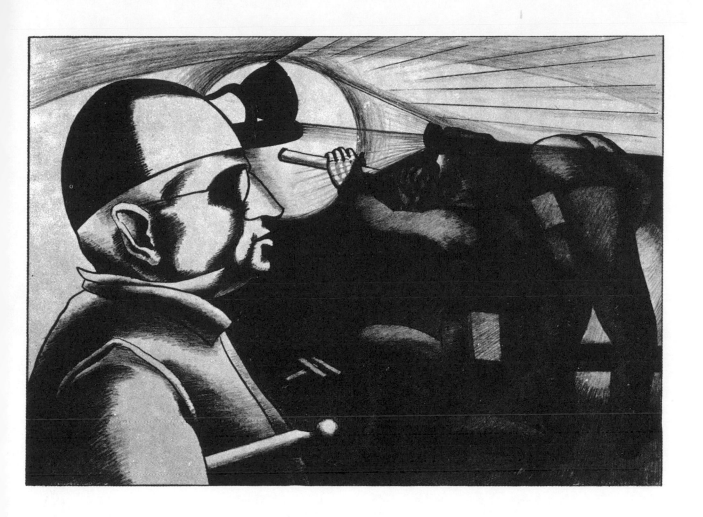

85
Mine Superintendent
Ernest Fiene

86
Civilization at the Crossroads
Jolan Gross Bettelheim

87
Insane Asylum
Bernard Sanders

88
It Can't Happen Here
Werner Drewes

89
14th Street
José M. Pavon

90
A Manhattan Landscape With Figures
Ida Abelman

91
American Scene
J. B. Turnbull

92
Strike
Emory Ladanyi

93
Dawn in the Assembly
Don Freeman

94
Trouble in Frisco
Fletcher Martin

95
Let 'Em Eat Cake
Dorothy Rutka

96
Road Workers
William Gropper

97
In Times of Peace
Morris Topchevsky

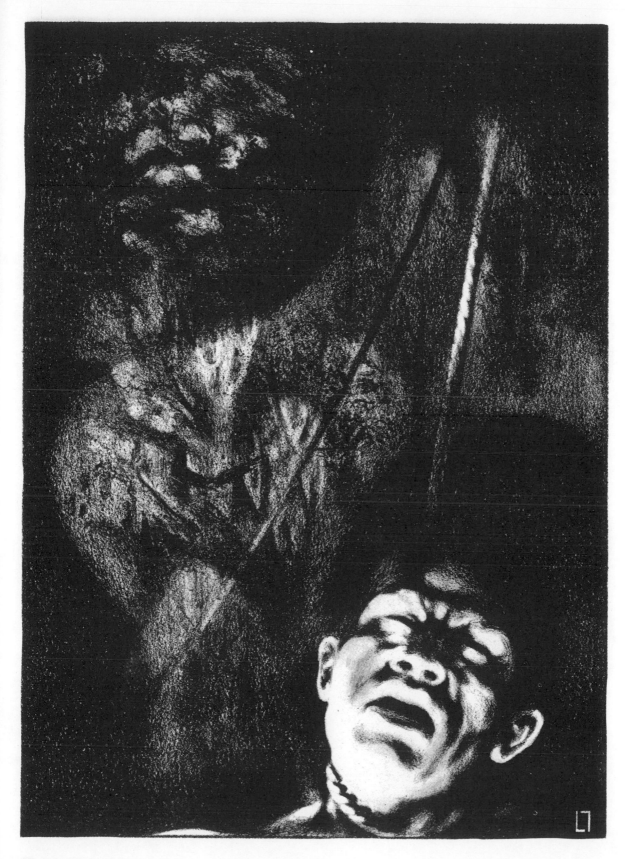

98
Lynching
Louis Lozowick

99
Company Town
Lynd Ward

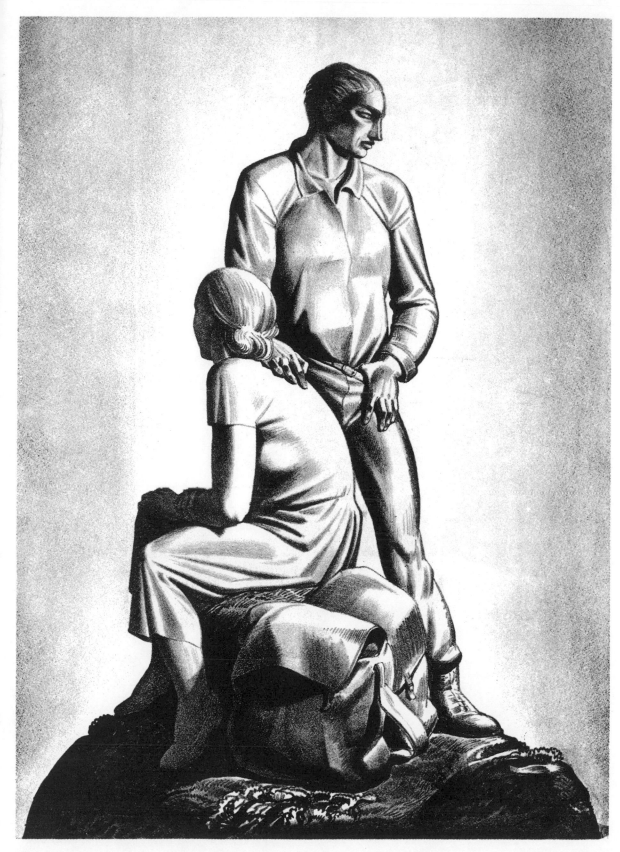

100
And Now Where?
Rockwell Kent